THE
SOCIAL
MEDIA
WHY

A Busy Professional's Practical Guide to
Using Social Media Including LinkedIn,
Facebook, Twitter, YouTube, Pinterest,
Google+ and Blogs for Business

By Crystal Washington

Published by McCarthy House Press, Houston, TX

Author Portrait: CJ Martin, *www.rmfoto.com*
Book Design: Mark Gelotte, *www.markgelotte.com*
Cover Design: Sherwin Soy

ISBN: 978-0-9892144-0-7
Library of Congress Control Number: 2013906519

ATTENTION: CORPORATIONS, PROFESSIONAL ASSOCIATIONS and ORGANIZATIONS:

McCarthy House Press books are available at special quantity discounts for use in corporate trainings, sales promotions or as conference materials. For more information, please contact Sales, McCarthy House Press, 2130A Holly Hall #211, Houston, TX 77054, (713) 383-9351.

For information on workshops; to book keynotes or to learn more about social media and mobile marketing, please visit *www.socialmediawhy.com*.

To My Ancestors,

Thank you.

Contents

Preface

Time is short these days, and there are many things fighting for your attention, so I am honored you decided to spend precious time reading this book. This book will provide you with clear insight into the most important business tools of our time! You are becoming a business professional of the future, taking steps down the path of relevancy and resilience. I hope to deepen and broaden your social media knowledge with the stories, information, and tips that follow.

Unless you've been stranded on the beach with your best friend Wilson for the past few years, you've heard of social media. You've likely been told by friends, family, and even strangers that it is the best thing since sliced bread. All these people are probably telling you to sign up for Facebook, Twitter, LinkedIn, and create your own YouTube videos on top of the blog you should start writing. But then what? What magic happens once you join? WHY should you care about social media?

What if I told you social media can make your life easier? In fact, it can land you a new job, help keep you and family members safe during a disaster, launch your small business, and even connect you with movers and shakers in your industry. Want to start a social movement? You guessed it—it's great for that too! **Social media can make you more efficient, effective, and connected.** Most importantly, it can open doors to new opportunities.

Social media is simply a tool. The user determines its effectiveness. Think about the microwave. Yes, there have been people who have microwaved cats. The results were less than pleasing. However, that doesn't make microwaves bad. Technology can be dangerous when used without understanding the how, when, and why of using it. Social media works the same way.

Social media is not magic, but it does connect people and allow them to build relationships. It's unique because it empowers you to connect with a greater number of people, with greater frequency, in less time than previously possible. However, you still build relationships the same way you do in person—over time. If you are looking for a quick fix to increase sales or a way to become an overnight success, social media is not for you. If you want to build lasting relationships that can turn into powerful business opportunities over time, you are in the right place!

My goal is to help you understand what social media is and is not, to help you determine what networks, if any, are a good fit for your needs, and to help you find practical uses for social media as a professional in the work world.

My Story

I have to start off by admitting I am an afro-puff wearing, earthy, tech-nerd from Generation Y. What makes me unique is that I'm a Gen Y with a dash of Gen X cynicism and Baby Boomer sensibility. While I value advancement and crave technology, I tend to think in terms of practical applications—how does a new piece of technology make life easier? How is this a better use of my time than that?

Social media enabled me to quit my job in corporate America to start a marketing firm from my home. Sites like LinkedIn, Facebook, YouTube, and Twitter helped my clients grow their businesses. I expanded my network of contacts, met amazing and inspiring people, and helped business owners and professionals use social media to find jobs, increase sales, and attract opportunities. The success I've experienced has enabled me to travel not only throughout the United States, but even to Africa and Europe as a speaker.

The ability to connect, foster relationships, and work with people is why I enjoy social media so much. Before it was popular to use social networks for business, I was in awe of the fact that in a matter of moments, I could connect with hundreds of people. Not only that, I could get to know them and build relationships. It may not seem like a big deal now, but it definitely was then.

After being urged to write a book on social media for the past four years, I finally decided to write the coolest, techiest social media book around. However, in the midst of writing it, more and more audience members at conferences asked me if I could recommend a social media book for beginners. Not just beginners, but professionals who may not be the most tech-savvy people. While there are many awesome books on social media—I've read many of them!—there is definitely a lack of books explaining social media in plain English for everyday people who just want to understand the practical applications.

Ah-ha! Suddenly, I realized I should write a book like that. So, into the garbage went all of the pages of work I had already completed. *Who am I kidding? There was never any paper, I typed it (Gen Y—remember?), but you get the gist.* So I rented a beach house for a few days to get away from technology in order to write a book on technology anyone could understand. As a result, I sit here writing as my afro blows in the sea breeze while cows graze in the distance. *(Did I mention I live in Texas?)* What follows in the next few pages is my heartfelt attempt to help everyday people incorporate social media into their professional lives.

As you read this book, remember it is ultimately up to you which actions you decide to take. If, based on the information I provide, you see a specific network will benefit you—use it. If not, save yourself some time and move on to the next one.

But whatever network(s) you choose, know that what you can accomplish, with a solid understanding and the right tools, is limitless!

Crystal Washington
Surfside Beach, TX
2013

How to Read This Book

This book is structured to give you an overview of the largest social networks used by busy professionals and how you can leverage them to become more efficient, effective, and connected.

If you are unfamiliar with popular social media terms, I suggest you read the Glossary first. If you're unsure of the value of social media, I encourage you to read through the entire book to gain a solid understanding of social media's practical applications. However, if you are just curious about a single network, feel free to skip to that chapter in Section 2. Read this book in the way that best suits you and your needs.

In the end, you will not be an expert, but you will have a solid understanding of the best social networks for professionals. There are plenty of amazing books that answer the WHAT and HOW of social media, and I recommend those books in the Additional Resources section. This book will explain WHY you should care about social media and what approach to take when using different networks.

Social media is constantly and rapidly changing. I've worked hard to ensure all information is accurate at the time of publishing.

SECTION 1
A Change Has Come

CHAPTER 1

Communication Shift

What is social media?

Social Media is simply a way to communicate interests; it is show and tell at its finest. Social media allows you to show, tell, and invite others to have conversations about your topic, interest, or brand. Your content may be with words, images, videos, or with a mixture of the above.

Social media is a communication medium. Prior to the home phone, how did people communicate over distance? They communicated via written letters. But how long does it take to write a letter by hand? And how long does it take for a note to reach its intended destination?

With the invention of the phone and its rapid spread through society, people were able to communicate with greater frequency and more efficiently. You could easily call in an order to a business versus sending an order form or letter. Can you imagine what happened to business owners of the early 1900s, who decided they did not want to get a phone because it would take more time to talk to people, and it was likely a passing fad? Many probably had to close their doors as the new innovation took over in the business world.

The phone did not replace the letter. However, it did allow for more frequent communication and reduced the number of letters sent.

Since then, the fax machine and email have also shifted the way we communicate, allowing for instantaneous, documented communication—the best of both worlds!

Now we have social media as well. Social media not only allows you to communicate quickly with a small or large number of people (depending on the size of your network), but also allows users to get a "snapshot" of other social media users. You can look on a new contact's Facebook profile and see who they are, what they care about, what projects they have taken part in, etc. Whatever they choose to share! In five minutes, I can communicate with twenty people on Facebook—commenting on their posts, liking something they've shared and posting my own messages. How long would it take you to call twenty people? How long would it take you to write twenty letters?

If you want to use social media for business, **use it to build business relationships**. In business, it is essential to remain "top of mind" with important contacts. You are more likely to be considered for opportunities, sales, business, etc., if a contact likes you and is used to communicating with you regularly.

In addition to building relationships, social media is used to leverage viral communications. For example, when mentioning a product, service, or idea, you may send a message to five people. In turn, they each send it to another five, and their contacts send it to the next five, so on and so forth. If a client has a positive experience with you or your business, you want them to recommend you on LinkedIn or spread the word about you on Twitter. In the end, you want the message to bring job opportunities, new business, or more mutually beneficial relationships.

It is not a numbers game. If you have a huge network, say 20,000 connections, but your online contacts never lead to offline action or sales— something is missing. At some point, you should meet contacts in person and speak with them; they should refer people to you, etc. It is better to have 100 contacts with whom you've built solid relationships than to have built an online network of 20,000 strangers connected to you for no apparent reason— what would be the purpose of that?

Social media is very different from traditional, older websites which only allow for one-way communication. Ten years ago, you went to a website and read what that company or site owner wanted you to read. That's it—one-way communication. Companies today that have a presence on sites like Facebook and Twitter have conversations with consumers. This benefits both the customer and company. One example is the story of Carl Larson and JetBlue.

In January 2009, JetBlue passenger Carl Larson was charged a $50 baggage fee for bringing a carry-on folding bicycle on a flight. According to JetBlue's bike policy, bikes would incur a $50 fee. Carl immediately took to Twitter, where his message was spread by bicycle enthusiasts until it was noticed by someone at JetBlue. Within 24 hours, the manager of Corporate Communications, Morgan Johnston, changed the policy, circulated the memo to all employees, and notified the public. Several other passengers were also refunded the $50 bike fee for folding bikes.

The above example is not unique. I have personally contacted airlines, software companies, and restaurants via Twitter to address product/service issues when traditional avenues were not helpful. In the end, great brands respond quickly and look for ways to make their companies shine. Of course, it doesn't hurt that possibly hundreds or thousands of people are watching the interaction on Twitter.

One of the coolest things about social media is that it levels the playing field. Anyone with a brand or idea in demand can create a large following, connecting to people locally, nationally, and even internationally. Anyone with a good plan and/

or large action-oriented network can influence a company, movement, or politics.

News is greatly influenced by social media. In fact, if a volcano erupts, the news will break first on Twitter and YouTube. Seconds after the blast, people will begin tweeting things like, "I'm running for my life. Mt. Volcano just exploded." On Twitter, you'll see a link to a video, taken by someone as they are running away from the lava. I don't know how (or why for that matter) they do it, but we live in an age when, even in danger, there will always be people who find the time to communicate with the rest of us via social media. Then the evening news runs their video. We now have the opportunity to get information straight from the source.

During the Arab Spring, I did not listen to much news coverage. Instead, I communicated with Facebook friends living in Egypt. One such friend, I'd met via Meetup (another social network) just prior to her moving to Egypt. Why watch the news when I could get a first-hand account from friends? They were limited to what they could say—apparently people who talked too much were "disappearing,"—but it was more reliable than second-hand news shared with a slanted perspective.

In the end, social media marks a shift in the way we communicate. People want to be able to connect instantaneously, share their opinions immediately, learn from each other, and get a window into the lives of friends and peers. Remember though, they can only see inside your house to the extent you open the blinds. You control what can be seen.

If you want to see really cool videos that highlight this shift in communications, I highly recommend Erik Qualman's YouTube videos. They can be found at *www.youtube.com/socialnomics09*.

CHAPTER 2

Same Rules, Different Venue

The rules of engagement online are exactly the same as offline. In other words, the same actions that work in creating great in-person relationships work online as well. The same actions that annoy people to no end in the real world will irritate online connections. Remembering this will give you more confidence in using social media and making wise decisions online.

Scenario #1 – As you are relaxing at home alone on your couch, you hear a knock at the door. You look through the peephole and see a man wearing a ski mask. He says, "Will you be my friend?" Do you let him in? Unless you have some really interesting family pranksters, probably not. In fact, for the sake of the person in the ski mask, I hope this does not take place in Texas, because he is probably going to get shot y'all.

While this may seem absolutely crazy, people do

it every single day. How is this any different from a person without a profile picture sending friend requests on Facebook or LinkedIn? Would it make you feel any better had the ski mask wearer also been wearing a company sandwich board? Probably not. Sooo ... do not use company logos for personal profiles. If you are connecting with me, you want to see a picture of Crystal Washington as my profile picture, not my company's logo—Socialtunities.

Scenario #2 – A new neighbor has moved into the neighborhood. You are having a Tupperware party at your home and have invited all of the ladies in the neighborhood. *I hope the men will bear with me through this example.* You plan to introduce the new neighbor to the guests. Everyone is sitting in your living room, enjoying delicious bites. You greet them and then introduce the new neighbor, Kathy. She immediately jumps up, pushes you out of the way, and then unrolls her business banner advertising that she's selling ladies shoes out of her trunk.

Seems silly, right? Well, this is what happens when you approve someone's friend request, and she immediately starts advertising herself or her products on your Facebook timeline, in the comments section of your blog, or on YouTube videos.

The things that are cheesy in real life look just as slimy online. Asking a new friend or connection to buy something as soon as you meet them, trying to partner with a new contact who does not really know you—they all smack of disingenuousness.

I want to introduce one last scenario that will demonstrate your responsibility on social media.

Scenario #3 – Imagine being gifted a beautiful luxury home for free. You decide to let everyone in, no matter who they are. After a while, your home is dirty and stinks, plus you are tired of the fighting and crazy conversations going on in your living room. It is obvious the house is stupid and is to blame for your situation, right?

In the above situation, that free luxury home is symbolic of your free social media profiles. While networks are imperfect, your experience will depend greatly on whom you choose to connect with.

To be successful on social media, consider how everything would play out in real life. If you are known as a knowledgeable, action-oriented person who is both giving and charitable—let that show on social media. Post about things that your contacts need or would appreciate more information about. Post events your friends would enjoy. Post about your charitable endeavors and how others can get involved. Connect your contacts with other connections who would be a good match.

To make things easy, I've identified the top five rules to help you.

Top Five Rules for Being Successful on Social Media

1. **Don't be weird.** Remember our assertion that the rules of engagement online are the same as those offline. Think back to scenario #1 above. Make sure you have a profile picture (and make it public) and fill in some information about yourself. If you are sending a request to someone you have not personally met, include a note explaining why you'd like to connect. Otherwise, you'll be known as the scary stalker person.

2. **Don't sell.** Social media is social! You have to interact with and engage people. Who wants to be friends with a billboard? The great thing about social media is everyone chooses when and with whom they wish to interact. People who are always selling or pushing some agenda are boring at best and annoying at worst. Imagine being at a cocktail party, observing different contacts holding conversations with an audience of people around them. You might walk around the room listening to conversations before you choose which ones to participate in. If you observe a boring, cheesy salesperson, you will likely tiptoe right past him/her and move on to the next conver-

sation. If you have a product or service to sell, build relationships by building yourself as an expert. Then, if you mention your offerings from time to time as a solution, it won't be seen as selling.

3. **Make a choice—business or personal?** You may decide to use social media to keep in touch with your eccentric great aunt or to build relationships with movers and shakers in your industry. Now, imagine your dream boss at the company you've been salivating over, seeing your aunt's post on your Facebook timeline about her latest body piercing. Probably not a pleasant thought, huh? You will have to make a choice. If your personal contacts are on social media for professional purposes, and you are certain they are not going to post inappropriate things on your timeline, you may add them. If that is not the case, do yourself a favor and don't add them. Some family members won't make the cut. I have a few of my own who I'll never accept a friend request from on Facebook. This doesn't mean I don't love them or won't communicate with them in other ways.

When I talk about making a choice, I do not mean that you talk only about business. At work, you may mention your children, a hobby, or even a cause you are passionate about. To build relationships, we have to let others see who we are—within reason. So, just as you do not share *everything* at work, you would not overshare online. Before posting, think, "Will this contribute to my professional image?" If it will build your personal brand as someone who is knowledgeable, kind, giving, a go-getter, etc.—go for it. If it will gross everyone out or anger people due to their personal beliefs—leave it out. This is especially true regarding political or religious posts.

4. **Be genuine.** The days of the phony business professional are over. The days of doing business with brands without getting to know the people behind the brands are over. Social media is social; people want to connect with real people. Take this opportunity to show a bit of your personality. Maintain a professional image while building relationships. Think about work relationships. Hopefully, you and your co-workers know something about each other's personal lives and personalities, even though you don't share everything. If you don't care for children, hopefully, you do not go to work pretending to be Fred Rogers or Shari Lewis. Sooner or later, people will figure out you are a phony. Imagine if you do manage to fool everyone in the office, but a

new person is hired who knew you before you adopted your current persona—a disaster in the making! Social media works the same way. This is not the time to reinvent yourself into a yoga-loving freethinker if you are really a Type A, Git-R-Done person. Eventually, if not immediately, people will see through you. When they do, you can count on at least one person announcing to the world, via social media, that you are not who you portray yourself to be. It makes much more sense to focus on being genuine from the beginning. Highlight your best features and care about others. Shower your connections with love!

5. **Add value.** The thing that separates someone who is on social media strictly for social reasons from someone who is on there for professional purposes is the fact that the astute professional will add value. Share your research/knowledge, link to great articles your contacts will find useful, keep your contacts updated on advancements, tools, and neat time-saving tricks. Connect your contacts with others who may be a good fit. Uplift someone who may need it. Make sure you are consistently leaving people you encounter a little better off than the way you found them. If you do this, people will start

to spread the word about you, and you will find yourself being connected to new friends, prospects, and potential collaborators.

CHAPTER 3

Not Your Teenager's Pastime

You may be thinking—"This is all well and good, Crystal, but specifically how will this help me?" Great question!

In Part 2, we are going to explore specific networks. But first, I want to give you an opportunity to write down all of the things that annoy you about social media, make you afraid of social media, or create negative feelings for you about using the sites. I'm serious, don't skip this; it is important! I'll wait for you.

_____

_____

_____

_____

_____

_____

_____

I've posed the question to many conference and workshop attendees, "What bothers you about social media?" These are the responses I hear most frequently:

I don't want to tell all of my business.

I was on there for a while, but my family kept posting annoying games, and I got tired of seeing my nieces' and nephews' inappropriate posts.

What can you possibly do on Twitter with just 140 characters?

I own a business; I don't have time to invest in social media.

I don't see how it applies to me.

It is destroying communication; I don't want to be a part of it.

It is a bunch of kids.

Social media gets people into trouble.

It is a waste of time.

I don't know where to start.

I know I should use it, but I'm not computer literate.

I prefer the phone or email.

Someone will rob my house or steal my identity.

What if I make a horrible mistake?

There are weirdos out there.

It scares me. I feel like I'm being left behind.

Now, review your own list. Do you have any of the common responses listed above? The truth is most people have the same concerns, fears, and frustrations about social media. Part of it is due to misinformation, part is due to lack of information available to non-techies, and a portion of it is true. **No matter what your concerns are, at this moment, they are all valid.** They are valid because, for you, they are real. The good news is you now have the opportunity to make decisions, based on real information, by taking fear out of the equation.

Statistics

Below are a few statistics that may surprise you about who is actually using social media, for what purpose, and the size of social networks.

One in six workers has used social media to find a job.[1]

18,400,000 Americans say Facebook got them their current job.[2]

8,000,000 Americans say they obtained their current job through Twitter. [3]

10,200,000 Americans say LinkedIn landed them their current job.[4]

98% of adults (18-24) online use social media.[5]

82% of adults (55-64) online use social media.[6]

One in every nine people on Earth is on Facebook.[7]

1. "2012 Social Job Seeker Survey," (2012), *Jobvite.com*, *http://web.jobvite.com/rs/ jobvite/images/Jobvite_JobSeeker_FINAL_2012.pdf*.

2. "Social Job Seekers Getting Ahead: Jobvite Survey Reveals One in Six Workers Successfully Used Social Networks to Get Hired," *Jobvite.com*, *http://recruiting. jobvite.com/company/press-releases/2011/social-job-seekers-getting-ahead- jobvite-survey-reveals-one-in-six-workers-successfully-used-social-networks-to- get-hired/*.

3. Ibid.

4. Ibid.

5. "98% of Online Adults 18-24 Use Social Media," *The Social Graf*, MediaPost Blogs, *http://www.mediapost.com/publications/article/ 160172/98-of-online-adults-18-24-use-social-media.html#axzz2OqZwMIEM*.

6. Ibid.

7. Steve Olenski, "Top Five Things I Resolve to Never Hear a Marketer Say About Social Media in 2012 ... And Beyond," *Social Media Today, http://socialmediatoday.com/steve-olenski/421588/ top-five-things-i-resolve-never-hear-marketer-say-about-social-media-2012-and-b*.

The average age of a social media user is 38.[8]

The average age of a LinkedIn user is 44.[9]

The median age of a Twitter user is 37.[10]

Eight out of ten LinkedIn users drive business decisions.[11]

As of December 31, 2012, LinkedIn counts executives from all 2012 Fortune 500 companies as members; its Corporate Talent Solutions are used by 86 of the Fortune 100 companies.[12]

34% of Internet users age 65 and older use sites such as Facebook and Twitter—and 18% of this group does so each day![13]

Based on the statistics above, you can see social media is being used heavily by adults, to help individuals find jobs, and to aid businesses to successfully connect with clients. Additionally, there is a good

---

8. Keith N. Hampton et al., *Social Networking Sites and Our Lives* (2011), Pew Internet & American Life Project, *http://pewinternet.org/~/media//Files/Reports/2011/PIP%20-%20Social%20networking%20sites%20and%20our%20lives.pdf*.

9 "Report: Social network demographics in 2012," *Royal Pingdom*, *http://royal.pingdom.com/2012/08/21/report-social-network-demographics-in-2012/*

10 Ibid.

11 "LinkedIn Audience in the US," *LinkedIn.com*, *http://marketing.linkedin.com/sites/default/files/pdfs/Infographic_LinkedIn_Audience_US_2012_0.pdf* .

12 "About LinkedIn," *LinkedIn.com*, *http://press.linkedin.com/about*.

13 Samantha Murphy, "Tech-Savvy Seniors: Half of U.S. Adults Over 65 Are Online," *http://mashable.com/2012/06/07/senior-adults-online/*.

chance any group of people you desire to connect with for professional reasons are using social media. Of course, the trick is to first locate them and then join only the specific networks they are using!

Double Trouble!

People have gotten themselves into deep doo-doo using social media. However, the problem is definitely the user, not the tool. Social media doesn't get people into trouble, people get people into trouble. We will tackle safety aspects in greater detail in Chapter 10, where you will see that you are in charge of what you share—the world will not instantly know everything about you. In the meantime, remembering the following five things will help you avoid destroying your reputation online.

Five Rules for Avoiding Social Media Hara-kiri

1. **Nothing is private.** This one is particularly hard for teenagers and politicians to understand. If you post a compromising picture of yourself or a really offensive comment on your private Facebook timeline or protected Twitter stream, the world still has access to it. Beyond hackers, all it takes is one contact/ friend/peer who is upset with you to take a screen shot of your post. What is a screen

shot? Have you ever noticed the Print Screen button on your computer? For many people, it is located near the function keys at the top of your keyboard. When you use this button, you can "take a picture" of whatever you are looking at on your screen. You can then paste it in a Word document, email it, post it in your own social media accounts, etc. Anyone can do the same to you. If you post something inappropriate or against your employer's social media policy and then delete it, the damage has likely already been done. We saw this repeatedly in the 2008 presidential campaign when vice presidential hopeful Sarah Palin's teenage daughters would post tweets and then delete them, only for major news outlets to have already captured screen shots.

2. **Think Granny Jumbotron.** If you wouldn't want your granny to see it or for it to be posted on a Jumbotron, don't do it. Ask yourself the following questions: Is it smart to post that politically charged message? Does the world really need to see your hairy legs and new Speedo? Is it really the best choice to post your home address if you work from home? Also, never post anything in a private message you would not want shared with the world. One reason is Rule #1 and the second

reason is that you could accidentally post something in a public area you meant to post in a private message.

3. **Bridle your inner Joan Rivers.** Joan has made a career being snarky and making fun of others. If you are not a professional comedian whose online brand revolves around a similar image, don't try it. Trust me, you'll look like a jerk, and people will unfriend or unfollow you.

4. **Social media is not a personal journal.** Maybe this seems obvious, but many people vent their frustrations on social media. I've seen people post amazingly private details about their intimate relationships, post about their bosses, and even request the wrath of a deity be brought down on someone's head. The truth of the matter is people have their own problems; they do not want to read about anyone else's. Additionally, who wants to work with or be around someone who obviously has anger issues? Sure, that doesn't mean the poster would attack them, but it does mean they allow their anger to supersede their common sense.

5. **Treat your social media profiles like your home or business.** I once had a client who

stated he had a very difficult time turning down friend requests and felt it was rude to do so. As a result, his Facebook timeline was packed with games, pictures of calendars, shoe advertisements, etc., all courtesy of his Facebook friends. I turned to him and said, "If a man knocked on your door, right now, and you saw he was wearing a zoot suit, platforms, a big fuzzy hat, and sporting a walking cane with two scantily clad women on his arms, would you let him in here—into the lobby of your business?" He laughed and said, "Of course not!" When I asked why, he answered, "Well, he'll make my business look less professional and may scare away my existing clients!" EXACTLY! If you accept any and everyone, it will eventually backfire and make you look bad in the eyes of the contacts you do want. I have seen Facebook timelines look like New York City subway cars at midnight—you see a little bit of everything, and I mean EVERYTHING!

Time

Social media can take a heck of a lot of time if you are just randomly checking accounts and making comments willy-nilly! Take a teenager's activities on social media, for example. Their constant updating is just how teenagers communicate. But that is not representative of all users.

Three-way calling was a big deal when I was in school. I distinctly remember a Saturday spent talking with seven friends (several of us had three-way calling) on the phone for five hours. What did we talk about? I don't know. I'm not even sure I knew then. We just had a compulsion to talk. Yet, this does not mean phones are a waste of time. It just means many teenagers have waaaaay too much time on their hands.

I think you would agree it is usually faster to drive to a destination than it is to walk. However, if you have a serious addiction to random joyriding, it may be faster to walk. The issue is not the vehicle; the issue is having a plan and *sticking with it.* In Chapter 9, I'll give you tools and tips for using social media efficiently, but be assured you can effectively use social media without falling into a time warp—you know, when people sign into Facebook at 8:15 a.m., and then look up and realize it is now 10:05 p.m. Oops!

Luckily, if you are concerned about time, you are not likely to be one of the people randomly cruising sites in the first place. You'll be a more strategic and purpose-driven social media user.

Mistakes

I constantly hear, "I'm afraid I'll make a mistake and mess up something." Here is the truth—**you will make mistakes.** You will accidentally delete a picture or post in the wrong place. Everyone has done it at some time. Give yourself permission to make mistakes.

The good thing is you are not likely to make huge mistakes because: (1) you are probably not in charge of social media for a large corporation; and (2) you have enough discretion and are now armed with the five tips listed earlier in the chapter to help you avoid personal brand suicide online.

Give yourself permission to make mistakes. If you follow the suggestions made in this book, you'll be fine. It's like parenting. You may forget to burp your baby, but it is highly unlikely you will mix up the Johnson & Johnson baby wash with chlorine bleach.

Killing Communication

I will never forget sitting in on a social media break-out session for professional speakers, listening to Scott Stratten of Unmarketing—I consider him to be one of the top experts on Twitter. As he shared amazing jewels on how he, his friends, and clients have used Twitter to get business, attract opportunities, and build great relationships, a woman raised her hand. He called on her. With a wry smirk, she said, "Where is all of this going? I see people walking around on their phones, texting, and not talking to each other. People are busy twittering and facebook-ing and all of that stuff while we are less connected than ever. Eventually, is everyone just going to communicate through Twitter and Facebook?" She crossed her arms huffily and waited for his response. To be honest, I don't remember what he said, though I do remember he was very gracious. I do, however, remember my thoughts in response to her statement. They were as follows:

1. Lady, you are destined to be one broke speaker. I get over half of my paid speaking engagements as a result of planners finding me online.

2. How are you going to stay relevant with younger generations, who will soon constitute the majority of meeting planners?

3. Your sarcasm doesn't mask your fear. It might make you feel better to pooh-pooh social media, but it doesn't change the fact professionals, especially in your industry, are having great success with social media tools.

Social media is changing communication as we discussed in Chapter 1. Maybe texting and social media are contributing to younger generations not knowing how to write very well. However, missing out on building valuable relationships, losing money, and wasting opportunities by protesting social media will not help youth write better or improve in-person communication.

Weirdos

Are there strange people online? Yes! However, the reason there are strange people on social media is because the world has its fair share of oddballs.

Simply ignore or block anyone undesirable on social media. You don't have to accept their connection requests, follow them, or reply to their messages.

Fear

I'm going to spare you a hyped-up pep talk and simply state the world is changing, and the ways in which we communicate have shifted dramatically. This does not mean you should throw out other means of communication. In fact, I would say that would be a huge mistake. It doesn't mean you have to join everything and sign up for every network your friends are on. That would be a HUGE mistake also because, honestly, many of your friends are likely wasting time. There are hundreds, if not thousands, of social media sites. But we're only going to look at a few of the biggest social networks best suited for professionals.

The important thing to remember is you are not late or even behind. Not everyone needs to be an early adopter. The first people to do things work out all of the kinks for everyone else. You have the opportunity to learn from those of us who have been using social media for a while. You get to avoid some of the mistakes we have made and get better results—faster. I would say that puts you in a pretty good position. All you have to do is be open to learning while using discernment to figure out what will work best for you and what social networks you may not need.

SECTION 2:
Meet the Networks

CHAPTER 4

LinkedIn

What is it?

LinkedIn is a powerful social network that helps you exchange knowledge, resources, career, and business opportunities with over 200 million professionals. LinkedIn is a cross between a resume bank, a yellow pages directory, and a business chat forum. LinkedIn gives you the ability to build and control your personal online brand, increasing the chances of influential decision-makers finding you on the Web.

LinkedIn is truly the no-nonsense social network. It caters to a sophisticated audience of career professionals. In fact, every Fortune 500 company is represented on the site. Another great thing about LinkedIn—it is the simplest to maintain. You don't have to worry about others posting things on your profile or posting numerous times throughout the day.

LinkedIn is the only social network where it is acceptable to make your profile 100 percent about you and your accomplishments. Think of it as a super-duper resume. You want to put your best foot forward to build credibility, getting others to weigh in on how awesome you are, and attract opportunities.

Over 200 million professionals are on LinkedIn, including CEOs, potential clients, friends, and any other type of professional you can think of. However, remember you *don't know most of these people.* **LinkedIn is not a place to go to immediately strike deals and sell people on you or your business.** Remember Social Media Rule #2 – Don't Sell. It is not like shooting fish in a barrel. People will report you and your account will be terminated. When you first meet someone, in person or online, they trust you enough to spend $0 with you and owe you zero favors. In other words, don't ask new contacts for anything, including a sale. Instead, just as in real life, focus on building relationships. If you build rapport by demonstrating your expertise, being helpful (giving first) and being consistent, those zeros will change over time.

Practical Applications

Use LinkedIn to find a job. As mentioned in the statistics in Chapter 3, over 10,200,000 Americans have reported finding their current job using LinkedIn. In fact, LinkedIn is the obvious choice for job search simply because it is the most professional social network. Using the Jobs feature in the menu bar, you can easily search for open positions by industry, company, or keyword. Additionally, you can follow companies on LinkedIn and receive email updates when a new position is posted.

Figure 04.01. Use the jobs menu in LinkedIn's menu bar to find open positions.

Increase the likelihood of being found by customers, influencers, and decision-makers. Whether you own a business or are a professional, you want to be findable. From an entrepreneurship perspective, LinkedIn is like the physical yellow pages from the 1980s. If you owned a brick and mortar business and were not in the yellow pages, you were missing out on business because people who were looking for your type of business would not find you. Similarly, if you and your business are not on LinkedIn, you will not be found on LinkedIn by potential customers, hiring managers, etc.

From a professional standpoint, recruiters

consider LinkedIn to be one of their best tools. According to one website, 93 percent of recruiters use, or plan to use, LinkedIn to acquire talent.[14] While I am not looking for employment, I have been contacted about many job offers by human resources professionals looking for "social media managers" and "marketing consultants." Maybe you are not looking to make a business move yet, but it does not hurt to dig your well before you are thirsty.

Find credible businesses. One of my favorite productivity tools is the search box on LinkedIn. Before, if I wanted to find a plumber, graphic artist or hairdresser, I had to use the yellow pages (online, of course) or ask friends. Now, I can simply type in who/what I'm looking for. The best part is I can then see if I know the person (maybe I forgot I have a contact who offers that particular service) or if there is a "friend of a friend" who offers the service. Then, I can click on the person's profile and see if any of my contacts have recommended them. If I see someone who is recommended by a few trusted contacts—I know I should use them. Now, I don't have to call anyone except the business.

Stay abreast of emerging industry trends. It is good to be in the know. By using LinkedIn Today (a collection of the most shared blogs and articles

14. "2012 Social Recruiting Survey Results," (2012), Jobvite.com, *http://web.jobvite. com/rs/jobvite/images/Jobvite_2012_Social_Recruiting_Survey.pdf.*

categorized by industry) and LinkedIn groups, you can stay on top of industry news, updates, great articles, and even join conversations with influencers. I recommend logging into LinkedIn for five minutes in the morning if you want to see any late-breaking industry news or great articles.

Figure 04.02. Use LinkedIn's search box to find desired contacts.

Reconnect with old business contacts. Everyone has lost touch with a good business contact. Perhaps you or he/she moved or switched companies. Unless you are a stalker, you probably would not feel comfortable tracking down the person's home address and showing up at the front door. However, LinkedIn provides a great, non-spooky way to reconnect. Simply type the name in the search box, or upload an old contact file. Or, using the advanced search option, type in part of the name and his/her past place of employment, and then see if you come up with something. If so, connect! While I'm sure you are memorable, be sure to personalize your connection request message just in case the person needs a little reminder of how you know each other. Without a personalized message, or picture, you are subject to being ignored.

Keep in touch with new contacts. Where are all of your contacts' business cards? If they are in a Rolodex, shoe box, plastic card carriers or anywhere other than uploaded somewhere digitally, you are doing yourself a disservice. The best way to ensure you'll stay in touch with contacts is to connect with them via social media. This way, you can keep up with each other between visits, calls, and emails. You can comment on their posts or send them messages when you see they've changed positions, companies, or added something to their profile. In Chapter 9, I'll give you tips on how to best upload your contacts into networks like LinkedIn.

Connect with fellow members of professional organizations between meetings. Many official organizations have also started LinkedIn groups. Some are public, others private. Either way, this can be a great way to connect with fellow members to ask questions, exchange information, and get input.

Save time collecting information. Have a question on how to structure a proposal, on industry standards, or if your target market will buy a new item? Post a discussion question or poll in a group. I recently saw a member of a meeting planners' group post a question about contracting. Within a day, several veteran planners responded with detailed information and even templates. Now that's value!

Figure 04.03. Post discussions and polls within LinkedIn groups.

Improve your search engine rankings. Have you ever Googled yourself? If not, I would suggest you try it. Type your name into Google and see what pops up. If you have a common name, you may see a variety of people, blogs, articles, and videos as results. However, if your name is a bit more uncommon, you may see your "evil name-twin," popping up all over the first two pages of search results. *Your evil name-twin tortures baby turtles while farting on butterflies for a living. Not good!* Or, you might find that picture of yourself which your ex-best friend posted on her blog. You know the one—where you are tipsy and moonwalking. Either way, you want the good stuff about you to pop up first. The great news is Google and other search engines love LinkedIn. Having a complete LinkedIn profile increases the chances a positive representation of you will pop up high in search engines. Results will vary based on how popular your name is. The more items on the Web with your name, the harder it will be to get on the first two pages of search engine results.

Prospect and eliminate cold calls. I used to be in sales, and I know, for most people, cold calling is about as much fun as a root canal. Who wants to call someone they do not have a relationship with to try to convince them they should have a business relationship? Yes, LinkedIn can help you here as well. Whether you are trying to connect with a potential client or a hiring manager, it is always better to get an introduction. Do you know the person's name and place of work? Assuming you know this information, use the search box to find the person you want to connect with. Then, click on his/her profile and look to the left to see if you have any mutual contacts. Here is where things get tricky—ready? **Do not use the "request an introduction" option on LinkedIn.** Instead, **pick up the phone** and call the mutual contact—you do know him/her after all, and say that you'd like to set up a lunch or would like to be somehow introduced to your

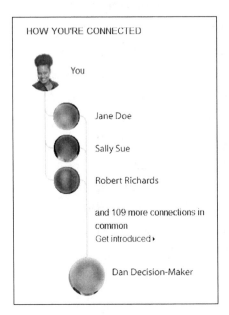

Figure 04.04.
LinkedIn allows users to view mutual connections between themselves and desired contacts.

desired new contact. Technology is great, but sometimes other forms of communication just make more sense. You can take this process up a notch with the advanced search option. Using the advanced search you can find the names of individuals holding specific titles at a specific company, in an industry, etc. It is the most powerful, yet underutilized, tool on LinkedIn.

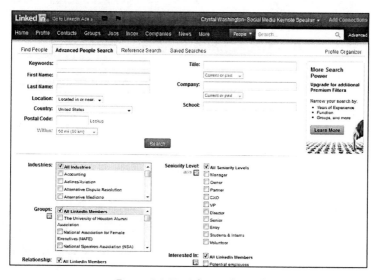

Figure 04.05. Advanced search screen on LinkedIn.

You may be wondering if it is necessary to pay for LinkedIn. While there would be a few more benefits to upgrading your account, most people do not even take full advantage of the standard, free version. For that reason, I'd suggest starting with the free version and working up to the upgrades should you need to access more search results, to see who is viewing your profile, or to post job opportunities for your company. LinkedIn ads can be a smart investment for business owners, but do not attempt to place an ad until you become comfortable with using standard features.

Top Five Action Items

1. Sign up to create an account on LinkedIn by visiting *www.LinkedIn.com*.

2. Fill out your profile completely, including your picture, current place of employment, contact information, headline, etc. If you want to use me as an example, visit my profile at *www.LinkedIn.com/in/crystalwashington*.

3. Upload your existing contacts. Go to *www.LinkedIn.com/fetch/importAndInvite*. If you need help getting your business card contacts imported into LinkedIn, see Chapter 9.

4. Join at least five LinkedIn groups that cater to your purpose/area of interest. Go to *www.LinkedIn.com/groups*.

5. Select your LinkedIn Today areas of interest by clicking the follow button next to your desired industries. This will determine what industry news will appear on your home page *www.LinkedIn.com/today*.

CHAPTER 5

Facebook

What is it?

With over one billion users, Facebook is the largest social network in the world. Facebook is a powerful relationship-building engine, perfect for attracting business referrals.

The one quality that makes this network the most valuable network for building relationships is the very quality that sometimes gives it a bad rap—it is the most social of the social networks. Unfortunately, sometimes users get too "social" and share inappropriate items.

To be successful on Facebook, you have to make your posts about your contacts and others. There is nothing wrong with talking about yourself, but be sure to use "we" more than "I." The best networkers are people who care about others and make them feel special. Well, if Facebook is the most social and social networks are about building relationships, then, of course, you need to highlight others and make them feel good!

Unlike LinkedIn which only allows a single profile picture or Twitter which only allows updates of 140 characters or less, Facebook allows you to post entire picture albums, notes, and much more! Of course, this also means there are many more ways you can get yourself into trouble if you are not careful about what you share and post.

Practical Applications

Use Facebook to find a job. 18.4 million Americans report finding their job via Facebook.[15] How can this be, considering that LinkedIn is "the professional" social network? The answer is simple—people do business with those who they know/like/trust. LinkedIn is great for finding people who are solid on paper, but Facebook is where you can go to get an overview of a person. In fact, according to a recent survey by CareerBuilder, over 37 percent of employers check applicants' Facebook profiles prior to hiring.[16] The number is likely much higher. You can be excluded

---

15. "Social Job Seekers Getting Ahead: Jobvite Survey Reveals One in Six Workers Successfully Used Social Networks to Get Hired," *Jobvite.com, http://recruiting. jobvite.com/company/press-releases/2011/social-job-seekers-getting-ahead-jobvite-survey-reveals-one-in-six-workers-successfully-used-social-networks-to-get-hired/.*

16. "Employers are Scoping Out Job Candidates on Social Media—But What Are They Finding?" *CareerBuilder, http://www.careerbuilder.com/ JobPoster/Resources/page.aspx?pagever=2012SocialMedia&template=none &sc_cmp2=JP_Infographic_2012SocialMedia.*

because of something on your profile, but you can also increase your chances of being hired by showing your expertise, using correct spelling and grammar, and having a sunny disposition. Facebook's Graph Search can also be a powerful tool in your job search. Know the name of the company you want to work for? Using Graph Search you can search for friends of friends who work for Company XYZ. Next step— ask your friends to connect the two of you!

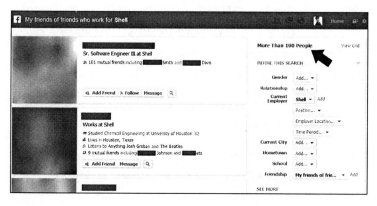

Figure 05.01. Facebook Graph Search query.

Connect with like-minded individuals. Facebook has pages, groups, events, and a host of other ways to connect with people in the same industry or with similar interests. Facebook is also a great place to find support groups made up of people from all over the world. If you are dealing with a tragedy or an illness, Facebook is a wonderful place to find support. Simply type the topic of interest in the search box and see what pops up. You can even narrow down the options to limit your search to just people, pages or groups, etc.

Stay first-of-mind with contacts. When opportunities, job openings or the chance to make a recommendation come up, you want your contacts to think of you. If you have not communicated with them in six months, your name will not likely come up. Facebook is a great way to quickly stay in the loop with your contacts. Comment on a picture or post they've shared. Recommend an article to them via their timeline or a message. Just stay in touch! I cannot tell you how many times I have posted a message on a friend's timeline to immediately have them call or message me about an opportunity.

Build deeper relationships with business associates/contacts. It is probably not appropriate for you to walk up to your director or vice president and ask, "Will you be my friend?" The same goes for that gatekeeper, or administrative assistant, at the account you are trying to win over. However, people are often far more willing to connect on social media than they are in real life. Once connected, comment on their posts and life events. Everyone wants to feel as though they are important. If you let them know you are interested, they will be more willing to help you, when the time comes.

Build your brand and following. On Linke-dIn, Google+, and Twitter, you can build your reputation as an expert. On Facebook, you build your brand. Facebook allows others to see your personality. Use this to your advantage. If you are an expert on childhood allergies and a breast cancer survivor/cure advocate—share that. You never know which other survivor might know a business, media outlet, or customer who might benefit from your expertise. If you are humorous or whimsical—show it. However, if you are not, don't fake it. Don't spend valuable time posting quotes all day (unless you add your own comments to them and they feed into your brand). Instead, focus on defining who you are, how you work with others, and how you can highlight and support your contacts.

Drive traffic to your blog/website/cause. Posting links in Facebook is a great way to drive traffic to other locations online. However, you cannot simply post a sale or put up links thinking if you do it enough, people will start to click on them. Add commentary, invite conversation, and do not be a cheesy salesperson. Ask your friends to comment on your blog posts or invite them to visit a link, telling them what to expect. Most importantly, hit emotional triggers. This is what causes people to take action on Facebook.

Keep an eye on _____ (fill in the blank). Sneaky, sneaky! Yes, Facebook is great for finding out what others are up to. Whether competitors, co-workers, superiors, or children—you can get a sneak peek into their lives (as long as their profiles are not set to private).

Drive action. I can think of no better example than the viral revolutions, also known as the Arab Spring in Africa and the Middle East that took place in 2011. Social media, specifically Facebook, did not cause the revolutions, but the network was a vehicle for organizing it.

Change.org was able to influence 1-800-Flowers to replace vendors using social media, especially Facebook. The organization sent out an email two weeks before Valentine's Day informing their list that 1-800-Flowers, the world's largest floral buyer, was not using Fair Trade Flowers. According to Change.org, this meant women and children were being physically and possibly sexually abused on flower farms. Those who received the email were then encouraged to sign the petition, email the VP of 1-800-Flowers, and/or let the company know their thoughts via their Facebook page. In a matter of hours, thousands of Facebook users posted their disapproval on 1-800-Flowers' Facebook page, vowing not to buy flowers from them for Valentine's Day. Within 48 hours, 1-800-Flowers agreed to change their policy and only buy Fair Trade Flowers beginning on Mother's Day, 2011.

If you have a cause that strikes an emotional chord, Facebook can be a wonderful catalyst, especially with a well-thought-out plan, as Change.org had in the 1-800-Flowers example.

Private or public? Allow posts or only comments?

I'm often asked if it is better to make Facebook profiles private or public. The answer is it depends on your purpose in using Facebook. If it is for business, it is almost always better to make it public so you can be found. However, if you are sharing somewhat sensitive information (remember—NOTHING is actually private), then you may not want to have your profile open to the world. You also have the option to allow others to post on your profile's timeline or only allow them to comment on things you've posted. I am never in favor of disallowing posts. Social media is built on two-way communication. Not allowing others the ability to post on your timeline is like telling someone who is visiting your home they are not allowed to introduce a topic of conversation—they may only speak on those things you have selected as appropriate topics. If friends posting games and other randomness on your timeline is what caused you to turn off the feature, then it is time to clean house.

Perhaps, you were not as selective as you should have been in the past, allowing in the entire midnight New York City subway crew. However, it is never too late to do a little spring cleaning. Besides, you don't want to stifle your ability to build relationships with great contacts because of a few rowdy characters who you should not have allowed into your house.

Personal profile or business page? Two profiles—one for friends, one for business?

Figure 05.02. Habitat for Humanity Facebook page.

Inevitably, business owners in my audiences ask if they should create a business page. This type of page is different from a profile because, rather than having "friends" it gets "likes." Compare this to real life. A person cannot be friends with McDonald's, but they can "like" it. For most professionals and even business owners, I do not suggest setting up a Facebook business page unless they develop a strategy (on paper) and have the time and resources to be consistent. While pages can prove successful, most business owners do not have the staff or strategy to create a successful Facebook following on a page. However, they do have the ability to build contacts via their own profile.

Figure 05.03. My Facebook profile.

Similar to real life, people don't care about your business until they care about you. If you do not like someone, you don't give a fiddlestick about late-breaking developments at their company. We live in a relationship age. People want to be connected to the people behind the brands. For this reason, it is easy for many professionals to gain personal contacts on Facebook, but much harder to get "likes" on a business page.

For a business page to be successful, it not only has to be engaging, it has to have what I call the "sexy factor." Is the topic/brand interesting? A mortuary should not have a Facebook business page. No matter how great the company's service, no one wants to keep up with the latest embalming techniques or hear how nice the late Mrs. Jenkins looked last week. The same could be said for insurance. Now, if you have a traveling taco truck or really unique jewelry—anything likely to gain a cult following—a page may be the answer. For everyone else, stick to profiles unless you are prepared to invest in professional help or in-depth learning of social media strategy for Facebook pages. Instead, build yourself as an insurance or death services expert.

A wonderful example of a great Facebook page is that of Barefoot Modiste, a company that specializes in making bohemian, ethnic, patchwork, and hippie clothing ranging in price from $30 to $250. This page has a little over 2300 likes—a respectable number—and a cult following that loves the pieces of clothing constructed like pieces of art. Once the owner finishes a new piece and posts it on her website, she shares a picture of the item on Facebook along with a link to purchase. Her connections then "share" the item on their own timelines.

Within hours, and sometimes just minutes, the piece is sold.

The second most popular Facebook question is: Should I create two accounts to separate personal from business contacts? My answer—No! First, it is against Facebook's terms of service (*www.facebook. com/legal/terms*), and one day, they will close both accounts. Additionally, it is only a matter of time before an influential person in your industry tries to connect with you via the wrong profile. Are you going to tell him/her to connect to your other account, not the one for friends? That is likely not going to help you build a better relationship. This is exactly why we have Social Media Rule #3—Make a Choice!

Top Five Action Items

1. Sign up to create an account on Facebook by visiting *www.facebook.com*.

2. Fill out your profile completely including your profile picture, cover photo, current place of employment, contact information, etc. Leave out any personal items you do not feel compelled to include. Be very careful to be respectful when filling out the political and religious section. Link to your website, LinkedIn profile, online resume, etc., if applicable.

3. Upload your existing contacts. Go to *www.*

facebook.com/find-friends. If you need help getting your business card contacts imported into Facebook, see Chapter 9.

4. Upload pictures that align with your goals for being on the network. This may be pictures of you at a networking event, pictures of industry events, your breast cancer walk team, you and your research team in Germany, etc. Personal pictures are okay if they add to your brand and do not detract from your professional image. For step-by-step instructions on uploading pictures, visit *www.facebook.com/help/?faq=174641285926169#How-do-I-upload-photos-and-create-a-new-album*.

5. Practice tagging friends on Facebook. When you mention people or brands on Facebook, you can tag them, making their name turn into a link to their own profile or page. As long as they have not changed their settings, your post will not only appear on your own timeline, but on theirs as well, increasing visibility! To tag a person, he/she must be your friend. However, you can tag any company or brand page. Start off by typing the "@" sign, followed by a user name. You will see a dropdown box where you can choose the friend's name. The "@" sign then goes away, and their name will remain highlighted in your post.

So, if you were my friend, and you typed, "Just finished reading Crystal Washington's book!"—you could tag me by using the "@" sign before typing my name. This would then appear on my profile for all of my thousands of friends to see. If any of this is confusing, simply visit YouTube and search for "how to tag on Facebook."

CHAPTER 6
Twitter

Twitter, tweeter, tweet? What is it?

Twitter is a powerful social network that acts as an efficiency tool to help professionals save time, identify key contacts, gain valuable information, and identify potential customers and job opportunities.

Twitter allows users to quickly and concisely express things that are important to them and connect with other people who value the same things. Notice the word "concisely"—because you only get 140 characters. That means people have to get to the point.

Figure 06.01. My Twitter profile.

Practical Applications

Use Twitter to find a job. Eight million Americans have reported finding their current job through Twitter.[17] If you are searching for employment, use Twitter to view job listings. There are many Twitter accounts dedicated to posting open positions submitted by recruiters. One such profile is @Microjobs. Twitter can also be helpful in demonstrating that you have a following—especially if you are applying for a position in the public eye or in marketing. Furthermore, you can connect with hiring managers and recruiters from specific firms and start to build relationships. But remember—ideally, you want to have a network in place before you need a new job.

Build business connections. Depending on your industry, you may be able to connect with peers, influencers, and experts online. When MD Anderson Cancer Center hired me to talk to their researchers about using social media, I showed them that many other researchers, experts, and hospital officials were using the network. While it may not be suitable for you to walk up to your VP and start a random conversation, you may discover he/she is on Twitter—it happens more than you think. Because they

---

17   "Social Job Seekers Getting Ahead: Jobvite Survey Reveals One in Six Workers Successfully Used Social Networks to Get Hired," *Jobvite.com, http://recruiting. jobvite.com/company/press-releases/2011/social-job-seekers-getting-ahead-jobvite-survey-reveals-one-in-six-workers-successfully-used-social-networks-to-get-hired/*.

are likely not amazingly popular on the network, they'll be tickled when you start to respond to their tweets, retweet them (share their posts), and even start conversations with them. When it is time for you to compete for a raise, and you and your competition stand with all things being equal, wouldn't it be beneficial for you to have an actual relationship with people in senior management?

Figure 06.02. Results for "society of women engineers" search on Twitter.

Conduct Research. You might be looking for information on a natural disaster happening right now, a conference in progress, or a particularly hot topic in your industry. Natural disasters often first break on Twitter. There is always someone on the brink of death—or running from it—who will take a few moments to tweet about it. News stations and newspapers often quote tweets now when they are covering a story that is unfolding. If you have a loved one in a danger area, Twitter is the best place to look for up-to-the-minute coverage. Simply use the Twitter search box to type in "Houston hurricane," "National Left Footers Conference," or "hypertension," for example, to get live updates and/or links to articles on a topic. The cool part is you do not need to have a Twitter account to use the search function.

Connect with like-minded people. Let's say you are passionate about the latest findings in the field of training and development—there is no better place in the world to go to find others with your passion than Twitter. Simply use the search box to find people who are talking about your interest. This can be professional or personal, including causes or even support groups for illnesses. Follow those people who are a good fit and send messages to them, comment on their posts, and share resources. If you provide good content in the form of tweets, other Twitter users will begin to follow you back. Being followed is a sign of influence. I've personally been hired for contracts as the result of Twitter followers, unknown to me outside of Twitter, recommending me to decision-makers in their organizations.

Make connections prior to conferences and events. Attending conference and industry meetings with few initial contacts is overwhelming for most people. If an event has a hashtag (they'll normally mention it on marketing materials and emails to attendees), you can type that hashtag (which starts with #) in Twitter and see all of the people who are talking about the conference. Start conversations with them, plan to meet up with them at the event, and create a network prior to arriving! For one of my personal examples, visit *http://youtu.be/iGHUAgMMZaY.*

Figure 06.03. Search Twitter for conference hashtags to connect with fellow attendees before the event.

Drive action or traffic to a website/blog. Like Facebook, Twitter can also be amazingly efficient at driving action. However, due to the brevity needed to post messages, you must direct people to websites, articles, or other online areas outlining the action steps needed.

A wonderful example of this would be "Tweetsgiving," which was started in 2008. It was the brainchild of an organization called Epic Change that was staffed by only two people, who took up the cause of funding a new school in Tanzania. Their goal was to raise over $10,000 in 48 hours. With the help of Twitter, a good plan, and a simple website, they were able to exceed their goal!

Top Five Action Items

1. Sign up to create an account on Twitter by visiting *www.twitter.com*.

2. Fill out your headline, add a picture, header image, and include a link to your website, online resume, blog, or another social network profile like LinkedIn or Facebook.

3. Customize your background and colors by choosing one of the alternate backgrounds or uploading your own image. Remember, make sure your background reflects the image you want to portray. Go to *https://support.*

twitter.com/articles/15357# for step-by-step directions.

4. Decide whom you want to follow. You can type in search terms, companies, job positions, or even names. Follow experts in your industry, potential clients, potential connectors, and anyone who you would like to follow you back. Do not automatically follow friends—only those who are posting items that you find of value. They may not use Twitter strategically, and their mundane posts could cloud your assessment of the network's value.

5. Become familiar with the "@"sign. The "@" sign allows you to tag people, similar to Facebook. The difference is the "@" remains at the beginning of your friend's name on Twitter. If you were to tag me on Twitter, you would say, "I just finished reading @cryswashington's book!" My Twitter name is cryswashington. This would allow your contacts to click on my name and see my profile. When you tag people, they tend to reciprocate, sending more people to your profile as well.

CHAPTER 7

Blogs

What is it?

Blogs are a powerful way to build your credibility as a topic expert, create an online following, and attract business and financial opportunities.

A blog is a collection of entries or articles created by one or multiple people, and it can be informative, educational, and/or entertaining. The entries can focus on a particular industry or topic, or may follow the life of an individual. Anyone can start writing a blog.

The two major benefits of a blog are that it can help solidify your status as a subject matter expert, and, secondly, search engines love blogs! Remember in LinkedIn when we discussed getting your LinkedIn profile on the first page of Google for your name? Well, blogs can help you do that with your name and area of expertise (depending on how competitive the topic is).

Blogs are not social networks like LinkedIn, Facebook, and Twitter, but are a part of the social media family. They allow people to come together based on a particular topic, and most blogs encourage commenting. This allows bloggers to not only give information, but be conversation curators as well.

Blogging requires both skill and time. If you are thinking about starting a blog, understand it is a much larger time commitment than keeping up with a social network profile on sites like LinkedIn, Twitter, and Facebook. You will need to constantly update your blog with new content. Some bloggers blog daily, while others do it as little as twice a month. Additionally, you'll need to work to attract visitors to your blog. Forget "build it and they will come," because "they" will not. You'll need to use other social networks, blog-sharing tools (social bookmarking), blog listings, and email marketing to get the word out. But no matter how frequently you decide to blog, you'll have to remain consistent. If you do not blog regularly, your readers will find other blogs and items to fill their needs and occupy their time, causing you to lose your audience.

Practical Applications

Blog to attract job opportunities. Having a well-thought-out blog on a specific industry topic can make you extremely attractive to recruiters. If they see you have a large Internet following—it's even better. In fact, some positions, like that of a news reporter, fit hand-in-hand with having a large online following you can drive to your work. With all other things being equal, do you think a newspaper publisher would hire a writer with no online followers or someone with over 30,000 active social media connections who can potentially click links to read his/her articles?

Build yourself as an expert and create a following. Being an industry expert with a large blog readership can, not only land you job opportunities, as mentioned above, but can also attract speaking, training, media, and collaborative opportunities.

Drive action. Are you trying to raise money for a nonprofit, bring awareness to a pressing industry topic, or encourage your peers to eat only locally grown, organic blueberries? There are thousands of blogs that focus on topics just like this and have made a positive impact on individuals, communities, and the world. You can provide support for a specific group—maybe dessert recipes for those living with diabetes. Bloggers have the power to use their space for good. Have you ever walked into someone's home and instantly felt comfortable, warm, and loved? You have the opportunity to make a "home" for like-minded, like-missioned individuals on your blog.

Improve your search engine rankings. One of the reasons search engines, like Google, love blogs is for the words contained in them. If you have a blog dealing with the subject of innovative leadership, you'll likely mention innovative leadership rather often. As a result, Google will know when someone types "innovative leadership" in Google Search; your blog is full of information on that topic because you've mentioned the term hundreds of times! The exact place where you come up in the results (#2 on page one, #7 on page 13) depends on a few factors, some of which are too techie for us to get into in this book. However, the competitiveness of the term— the amount of other blogs, websites, videos, etc. devoted to it—will also influence how high you rank, and it can vary from day to day.

Read other blogs to stay on top of industry/ topic developments. You don't have to have your own blog to benefit from blogs. There are many amazing blogs that can help you stay abreast of late-breaking developments in your industry. You can even have new posts delivered into your inbox by pushing the little button that looks like three quarter circles on your blog of choice. Note: Not all blogs have this button for RSS (really simple syndication).

 Figure 07.01. RSS symbol.

Make money. While this is not an option for casual bloggers, career bloggers often sell ad space, memberships, and even attract sponsors. If you have a passion like travel, are a good picture-taker, have an engaging personality, and are willing to study the art of blogging, you can create a decent income with a professional blog.

Action Items

1. Decide if you want to use a free blogging site, or if you would like to have a blog on your own private website. The first is free to set up, but the latter allows you greater control of its look and feel, and gives you the ability to drive more traffic to your website, helping you grow your own brand (versus the brand of the free blog service). If you want a free blog, consider visiting *www.blogger.com* or *www.wordpress.com*. If you want a blog on your own website, contact a web designer. I suggest you tell your web designer you would like a WordPress site. This is different than the free one, but uses the same technology, making it easier for you to maintain and update once your web designer sets it up for you.

2. Add links on your blog to all of your social media profiles.

3. Email your contacts, letting them know about your new blog, once it is ready for viewing.

4. Begin reading CopyBlogger *(www.copyblogger. com/blog/)* and ProBlogger *(www.problogger. net)* for blogging tips and tricks!

CHAPTER 8

Others Worth Mentioning

YouTube

YouTube is a hugely popular social network that allows users to share, comment on, and perform minor editing of videos. Over one billion unique users visit YouTube each month with over 72 hours of video added every minute.[18] YouTube has radically changed the way people search online. In fact, it is the second largest search engine. Do you want to learn how to set up payroll in Quickbooks or post a new picture on Facebook? I assure you there are several videos on the topic. If there is something you do not know how to do, online, or in "real life," there is likely a video offering step-by-step directions. YouTube is a new social media user's best friend. Want to know how to stop receiving emails from Twitter? Type "how to stop Twitter emails" in YouTube's search box.

---

18. "Statistics," YouTube, *http://www.youtube.com/yt/press/statistics.html.*

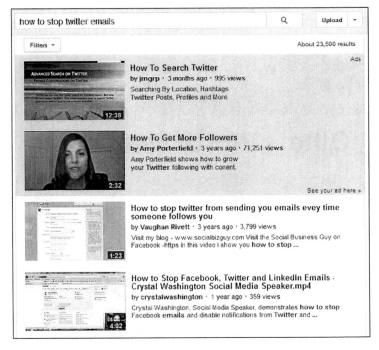

Figure 08.01. YouTube search results.

Creating a YouTube account is fairly easy. If there are any YouTube users who post particularly helpful videos, you can subscribe to their channel and receive updates each time they post a new video. Of course, you can always post your own videos as well. This can help build your credibility as an expert, and if you title your video well and create a complete description, it may improve your rankings on Google for the words you have included in your video's title and description. Lastly, it can help you create more great content to share on your blog and social networks.

Google+

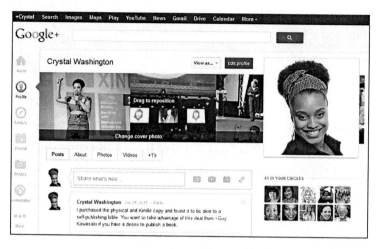

Figure 08.02. My Google+ page.

Google+ is the baby on the list. Released in 2011, it has been one of the fastest growing networks of all time, now having over 500 million registered users. However, in terms of daily activity, it is still lacking. The average user spends 3.3 minutes monthly on the network.[19] In other words, many people sign up, but do not log in on a regular basis. Google+ users use the network to build their status as experts and share valued content. If you find Facebook updates to be mundane, Google+ is where you belong. Google+ is where the smart people hang out and share great content and information. If Facebook is about creating

---

19. Erika Morphy, "Dear Google, It's Not You, It's Us," *Forbes, http://www.forbes. com/sites/erikamorphy/2012/03/03/dear-google-its-not-you-its-us/.*

community, Google+ is where you go to find brilliant people who share your passion. The jury is still out on Google+, with social media experts extremely divided on the topic. It is my belief that, while Google+ certainly adds value, most professionals who are social media newbies will not find a great deal of usefulness for it. Primarily, it is because people who they are looking to connect with are not using the network consistently. Yet, this network bears mentioning for three reasons:

1. Google owns it! This means that creating a profile can increase your rankings on Google.

2. It is a great place to find information. Most of the users who do engage regularly are topic experts with a strong desire to share useful information.

3. If you are looking to connect with young men in the technology industry—this is the place to be! The network is dominated by men (71 percent).[20]

---

20. Fiona Menzies, "Women Are From Pinterest, Men Are From Google+?" *Forbes, http://www.forbes.com/sites/gyro/2012/08/20/women-are-from-pinterest-men-are-from-google/.*

Pinterest

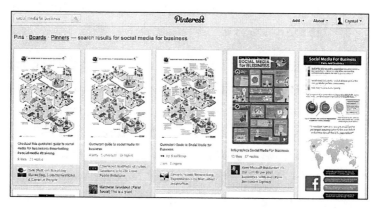

Figure 08.03. Pinterest search results for "social media for business."

Pinterest, another fast growing social network that took the Web by storm, is extremely unique for two main reasons—it has a 82 percent female user base[21] and drives more referral traffic and sales than YouTube, Google+, and LinkedIn combined![22] Users "pin" images on virtual pinboards, allowing followers to repin, share, and comment on their pins. Here's what you need to know:

1. This network is definitely worth visiting if you have a "visual brand." If you sell homes,

---

21. Britney Fitzgerald, "More Women On Facebook, Twitter And Pinterest Than Men," *Huff Post Tech*, Huffington Post, *http://www.huffingtonpost. com/2012/07/09/women-facebook-twitter-pinterest_n_1655164. html?utm_hp_ref=women&ir=Women.*

22. Janet Aroncia, "Pinterest Drives More Referral Traffic Than Google Plus, YouTube and LinkedIn Combined," *Shareaholic, http://blog.shareaholic. com/2012/01/pinterest-referral-traffic/.*

knitted cup holders, jewelry, etc.—Pinterest is where you want to be.

2. If you are a meeting planner, primary school educator, or do any type of collaborative work that includes visual elements, Pinterest may be a good option for extended project collaboration and input. Simply create a group board (can be private—called "secret"—or made public) and begin sharing.

3. Pinterest drives more sales than other popular social networks. A person who clicks on one of your pictures on Pinterest (causing them to go to your website) is more likely to buy from you than someone who visits your website via a link from Facebook or Twitter!

One word of caution—be careful to post only images you own the rights to, observing copyright licenses!

SECTION 3:
Take Action

CHAPTER 9

Moving Forward

Now that you have reviewed the top social media and social network options, decide which ones are best for you. You may feel, based on the practical applications, LinkedIn and YouTube would be the best suited for you. On the other hand, if you are looking for a new position, you may want to use LinkedIn, Twitter, and Facebook. Make your decisions and move forward. You can always add another network later, should you choose.

Review of Top Action Items

In Chapters 4-7, you were given top action items for each social network. Choose your selected social network below and check off each action item under your chosen networks, as you complete them.

LinkedIn

▶ Sign up to create an account on LinkedIn by visiting *www.LinkedIn.com*.

▶ Fill out your profile completely including your picture, current place of employment, contact information, headline, etc. If you want to use me as an example, visit my profile at *www.LinkedIn.com/in/crystalwashington*.

▶ Upload your existing contacts. Go to *www.LinkedIn.com/fetch/importAndInvite*.

▶ Join five groups, based on your purpose/area of interest. Go to *www.LinkedIn.com/groups*.

▶ Select your LinkedIn Today areas of interest. This will determine what industry news will appear on your home page at *www.LinkedIn.com/today*.

Facebook

▶ Sign up to create an account on Facebook by visiting *www.facebook.com*.

▶ Fill out your profile completely including your profile picture, cover photo, current place of employment, contact information, etc. Leave out any personal items you do not feel compelled to include. Be very careful to be respectful when filling out the political and religious section. Be sure to link to your website, LinkedIn profile, online resume, etc., if applicable.

- Upload your existing contacts. Go to *www.facebook.com/find-friends/*. If you need help getting your business card contacts imported into Facebook, see the section in the chapter named Connecting with Your Business Card Contacts on LinkedIn, Facebook & Twitter.

- Upload pictures that align with your goals for being on the network. For step-by-step instructions, visit *www.facebook.com/help/?faq=174641285926169#How-do-I-upload-photos-and-create-a-new-album.*

- Practice tagging friends on Facebook. Start off by typing the "@" sign, followed by their name. You will see a drop-down box where you can choose the friend's name. The "@" sign then goes away, and his/her name will remain highlighted in your post.

Twitter

- Sign up to create an account on Twitter by visiting *www.twitter.com.*

- Fill out your headline, add a picture, and include a link to your website, blog, or another social network profile like LinkedIn or Facebook.

- Customize your background and colors by choosing one of the alternate backgrounds or by uploading your own image. Remember, make sure your background reflects the image you want to portray. Go to *https://support.twitter.com/articles/15357#* for step-by-step directions.

- Decide who to follow. You can type in search terms, companies, job positions, or even names. Follow experts in your industry, potential clients, potential connectors, and anyone who you would like to follow you back.

- Become familiar with the "@"sign. The "@" sign allows you to tag people, similar to Facebook. The difference is the "@" remains at the beginning of your friend's name. When you tag people, they tend to reciprocate, which sends more people to your profile as well.

Blog

- Decide if you want use a free blogging site or if you would like to have a blog on your own private website. The first is free to set up, but the latter allows you greater control of the blog's appearance and will drive more traffic to your own website.

- Add links on your blog to all of your social media profiles.

- Email your contacts, letting them know about your new blog, once it is ready for viewing.

- Begin reading CopyBlogger (*www.copyblogger.com*)

and ProBlogger (*www.problogger.net*) for blogging tips and tricks!

Others

▶ **YouTube:** Visit YouTube for great how-to and informational videos. Create an account at *www.youtube.com*.

▶ **Google+:** Create an account at *http://www.plus.google.com*.

▶ **Pinterest:** Create an account at *www.pinterest.com*.

Using Apps

Each of the social networks mentioned in this book have mobile apps for smartphones and devices. These apps allow you to use the networks in a more user-friendly format that is faster than accessing the full website version from your device. If you use an Android phone, iPhone, or tablet that runs on Android or iOS, you may want to consider downloading the free apps for your chosen social network to allow for easier access and updating from your mobile phone. Be sure to closely review the terms of service for each app as some require gaining access to your phone's contacts or may have other terms you may not wish to allow.

Uploading Business Card Contacts

It is pretty simple to upload contacts into Facebook and LinkedIn from email accounts. Business cards, however, are not so easy—unless you have time to type email address after email address in a little box.

Where is the information from your contacts now? Do you have business cards in a Rolodex? Perhaps, you are in the position I was in a few years ago—with a tub of cards. Yes, I said, "tub." The fact of the matter is you are three times more likely to interact with a contact whose information you have stored digitally rather than with someone whose business card is shoved in the back of your desk. Luckily for you (or your assistant), inputting contact information, and staying in contact with new connections, is now easier than ever. So, get that tub-o-cards out, and I'll share three of my favorite resources for inputting contact information, as well as how to connect with your contacts using three large social media networks: LinkedIn, Facebook, and Twitter.

Three Tools for Converting Business Card Contacts into Digital Contacts:

1. **Cardmunch** (*www.cardmunch.com*)—if you have an iPhone, this free and easy-to-use app will allow you to take a quick picture of a card

that will then be transcribed and uploaded into LinkedIn. This is great for those contacts who you want to immediately connect with on LinkedIn.

2. **Google Goggles** (*https://market.android.com/ details?id=com.google.android.apps.unveil &hl=en*)—this free Google service is similar to Cardmunch, but for those with Android phones. Simply take a picture of the business card and save it to your contacts! Easy!

3. **Shoeboxed.com** (*www.shoeboxed.com*)—this is my favorite option! Why? Because I simply throw all of my cards into a prepaid envelope, virtually indestructible—except when encountering pyromaniac mail carriers. And I receive a link to download my contacts' information a few days later. Certain plans include the cards being returned to you. I can then upload the contact file they produce into Outlook, LinkedIn, Twitter, or Facebook. With plans less expensive than a large pizza, this is definitely, in my opinion, the best option for inputting those contacts who you do not need to immediately contact (i.e., the tub-o-business cards). Plus, it is much more cost effective than paying an assistant to do it. Sometimes they even offer free trials.

Connecting with Your Business Card Contacts on LinkedIn, Facebook & Twitter:

You now know how to convert your business cards into a digital format. In order to connect with your contacts, you'll need to convert the information into .CSV format.

If you use Shoeboxed (my favorite service), it will already be in that format.

If you used Cardmunch, you can export your contacts into .CSV format by logging into your account and selecting Contacts > Connections > Export Connections (bottom right).

If you used Google Goggles, you can export your contacts from Gmail by logging into your Gmail account and selecting Contacts > More > Export > Outlook CSV Format.

If you happen to already have contacts in Outlook you want to connect with via social media, go to File > Import & Export > Export to a File > Comma Separated Values (Windows) > Contacts > Next > Finished.

Once you have your .CSV files, you can now connect with your contacts via social media!

How to Connect with Contacts on LinkedIn

1. Log into LinkedIn.

2. Contacts > Add connections

3. Select Any Email

4. Choose Upload contacts file

5. Select your file, and then choose Upload. Select the contacts you wish to invite—I suggest only those with the LinkedIn symbol by their name, meaning that they are already on the network—and then choose "Send Invitations."

How to Connect with Contacts on Facebook

1. Log into your Facebook account, and then go to *https://www.facebook.com/invite.php*.

2. Import Your Email Addresses > Other Tools.

3. Scroll down to the bottom until you see the box to upload your contacts. Select the file and then choose "Upload Contacts."

How to Connect with Contacts on Twitter

Twitter is a little trickier than LinkedIn and Facebook when it comes to uploading your contacts' information.

1. Log into Twitter.

2. Who to Follow > Find Friends.

3. You will have to use Gmail, Yahoo, MSN, or AOL to upload your contacts. You can simply upload your CSV file into any of those email services to import your contacts into Twitter.

4. Whew! Now your contacts are digital and easily accessible. Time to build relationships!

Posting Frequency

Wondering how often you should post on each social network? While it varies by user and purpose, I would recommend the following to start off. Then adjust according to the amount of responses, comments, and clicks you receive.

LinkedIn – One time every one or two days, or link to your Twitter account if your Twitter postings would be appropriate for the strictly professional network.

Facebook – For your profile page, one to three times per day. If you have a business page or group, once every other day for those.

Twitter – Four to six times per day.

Blog – One to two times per week.

Efficiency & Measurement Tools

If you have decided to use one social network, managing it on a regular basis may not seem like a huge task. However, if you have decided you should use three social networks, and you have previously been on none, that may seem like a bit of an undertaking.

The good news is you don't have to do all of this at once. You may decide to add one network a month, until you are on all three. The important part is to get started and use the action items suggested in this book.

But wait! I have more good news. There are tools out there that can make managing multiple social media accounts easy. One of my favorites is Hootsuite (*www.hootsuite.com*). Hootsuite allows users to update multiple accounts from one place. Additionally, you can schedule future posts. For instance, if you see three articles you would like to share today on Twitter and LinkedIn, you can schedule the date and time they will go out to your friends, followers, and contacts. Another awesome function of Hootsuite is it allows you to see how many people click on your links to websites, articles, etc. You could create the following post in Hootsuite: "My latest blog post is on 'Five Things Everyone Should Know

About Heart Disease' at www.heartdblog.com."
Hootsuite will send out something like the following: "My latest blog post is on 'Five Things Everyone
Should Know About Heart Disease' at http://
ow.ly/8k6326." It will shorten your link, but it will
still go to your desired site. Then, you can see how
many people clicked on the link. This is extremely
important because you can see how interested your
connections are in what you are posting. You can also
track what types of posts are most appealing. Lastly,
you can manage your Facebook, Twitter, and LinkedIn accounts from within Hootsuite—commenting
on posts, liking items, and even viewing videos. If
you have a smartphone, iPhone, or Android, you can
even use Hootsuite from your phone.

Another resource to consider for managing and
updating multiple networks is Social Oomph. It
does not have all of the features of Hootsuite, but
it can be used to update multiple networks via any
phone—even those without Internet access. It uses
the same technology as text messaging.

If you have a blog, consider using Google Analytics (*www.google.com/analytics*). This will help you
track the amount of traffic you receive to your blog,
know how people are finding it (is it through searching search engines or from your Facebook page),
what posts are most popular, how long readers stay,
etc. All great information to know!

Stay Productive

I'll be the first to admit, falling into a social media black hole is something we all do. I've had more than my share of days when I've started off uber-productive only to find three hours have passed, and all I have to show for it is a gazillion interactions with Facebook friends, and many laughs.

Want to become productive on social media? Here are my recommendations:

1. **Make a Plan.** Understand exactly who you would like to reach (your target markets) and design your brand in a way that will be attractive to this group. Do not simply post what you want people to read, post what they want to read. Make a conscious decision to post information that appeals to your target markets vs. what you want them to want.

2. **Sign up for Google Alerts and visit Alltop.** Google Alerts (*www.google.com/alerts*) will send you emails about specific topics you would like to post about. Simply type in the search words and set a new alert. Alltop (*www.alltop.com*) has hundreds of categories to choose from. Simply click on the link for your topic to instantly see top blog posts and articles you can share via social media.

3. **Create a Posting Calendar.** Use a blank calendar (*www.office.microsoft.com/en-us/templates/ results.aspx?qu=month+calendar&ex=1*). Decide what you're going to post on social media each day, and then fill in your calendar with your choices. Consider holidays, upcoming events, and other items that might influence your posting. You can also include your blog, if you'd like. Do this at least a month ahead of time.

4. **Sign up for Hootsuite.** Hootsuite will allow you to update your social networks from one place. Additionally, you can schedule future posts on Facebook, LinkedIn, and Twitter.

5. **Buy a kitchen timer.** Decide exactly how much time you will commit to social media each day. I suggest 10-20 minutes in the AM and maybe 10 in the PM. At whatever time allotted each day, set your egg timer for the correct amount of time. Then use that time to post, moderate, comment on others' posts, photos, etc.

CHAPTER 10

Staying Safe

Settings

One of the best ways to stay safe online is to familiarize yourself with your privacy setting on each network. You can view and adjust the settings of your accounts at these links:

LinkedIn: *www.LinkedIn.com/settings* (see privacy controls)

Facebook: *www.facebook.com/settings* (see security) and *www.facebook.com/settings/?tab=privacy*

Twitter: *www.twitter.com/settings*

YouTube: *www.youtube.com/account*

Google+: *www.google.com/settings/plus?ref=home* (select Google+)

Pinterest: *www.pinterest.com/settings*

Top 7 Rules for Staying Safe on Social Media

1. Do not post your home address on any social media account.

2. Do not post your year of birth on your social media accounts.

3. When using check-in or location-based social network features (e.g., Facebook), only check in as you are leaving a venue.

4. Use a different password for all social media accounts and be sure not to use the same password for your banking or sensitive accounts.

5. If you receive an email from a social network, hover over the link before clicking on it to be sure it is valid and it is not trying to scam you into giving your login information.

6. Do not accept friend requests from suspicious-looking accounts.

7. Do not click on any sensational social media posts saying things like "I can't believe you did this in this picture" or "You will not believe what he did to_____." Delete those posts from your timeline, and tell your friend/contact who originally posted it that their account has been hacked. You might want to unfriend them until the problem is fixed.

CHAPTER 11
Be an Explorer!

If I come in there and find it, you are in big trouble!
—Katharine Washington (my mother)

Experts are awesome, but you don't need one to guide your every step. If you are wondering how to do something on social media, type your question into Google or, if you'd like a visual, search YouTube. Don't be afraid to research things for yourself. You'll be surprised how many answers are right at your fingertips.

I credit my mother with encouraging me to be curious and take the initiative to look for things myself—even if the encouragement did come as a threat at times. As a result, I've fixed phones, televisions, my car, and even found homeopathic cures for my own body. I'm certainly no repair woman or doctor, but I've saved myself a great deal of time and money over the years. When something is serious, I call in an expert.

Give yourself permission to try out new networks,

create profiles, click on buttons, and, most importantly, make mistakes! Use this book as a guide to help you make good decisions, but feel free to take your social media usage to the next level. When you become comfortable, try a new network, or try a new feature!

Additional Resources

You understand the practical applications of social media, have enough information to make informed decisions, and are, hopefully, comfortable enough to look around and try different networks. You may want to read further for more in-depth information on social media and strategies. Below, you will find just a few of my favorite books and resources that will help you get a deeper understanding of social media, specific networks, and creating a strategy.

Books

Evans, Dave, and Susan Bratton. *Social Media Marketing: An Hour a Day.* Sybex, 2012.

Gitomer, Jeffrey. *Social BOOM!: How to Master Business Social Media to Brand Yourself, Sell Yourself, Sell Your Product, Dominate Your Industry Market, Save Your Butt, ... and Grind Your Competition into the Dirt.* FT Press, 2011.

Hall, Star. *The Social Wave: Why Your Business is Wiping Out with Social Media and How to Fix It.* Entrepreneur Press, 2011.

Kabani, Shama. *The Zen of Social Media Marketing: An Easier Way to Build Credibility, Generate Buzz, and Increase Revenue.* BenBella Books, 2013.

Kawasaki, Guy. *What the Plus! Google+ for the Rest of Us.* McGraw-Hill, 2012.

Meerman Scott, David. *How to Use Social Media, Online Video, Mobile Applications, Blogs, News Releases, and Viral Marketing to Reach Buyers Directly.* Wiley, 2013.

Stratten, Scott. *UnMarketing: Stop Marketing. Start Engaging.* Wiley, 2012.

Treadway, Chris, and Mari Smith. *Facebook Marketing: An Hour a Day.* Sybex, 2012.

Blogs & Websites

www.mashable.com/social-media
www.socialmediaexaminer.com
www.social-media.alltop.com
www.copyblogger.com/blog
www.problogger.net

Glossary

In this section, you will find a list of social media related terms used in this book.

A symbol appearing at the beginning of a hashtag on Twitter and Google+; used to find posts about specific topics.

@   A symbol used to tag another social media user on a social network that turns their name into a link to their profile while alerting them to view the post.

Blog   A website where a single user or multiple users share experiences, content, or other information, normally centered on a specific topic or theme.

Board   A collection of user pins with a specific theme on Pinterest.

Cardmunch   An iPhone app that allows users to take pictures of business cards and easily upload contact information from them into LinkedIn.

Comments   Responses left by other users on a social media post.

Facebook   A social network, with over one billion users, that allows users to post pictures, create posts, send private messages, participate in groups, and much more.

Feed   A constantly updating list of posts from your connections on social media sites.

Follow   The ability to see posts from a social media user on social networks; the user may or may not elect to see your posts.

Friend   A social media connection.

Google Analytics   A free tool that allows users to track website user data, including what websites users are coming from, how long they visit specific pages, and more.

Google Goggles   A free Android app that allows users to take pictures of business cards, landmarks, barcodes, etc.; users can then upload business card contact information to their computers, or find useful information about other items via Google's database.

Google+   Google's social network; often compared to Facebook.

Group   A type of private or public page created in social networks like Facebook, LinkedIn, and Google+ that users can join based on a common interest or affiliation; users can communicate with other group members.

Hashtag   A word starting with the symbol "#" on social networks; used to find posts about specific topics.

Hootsuite   A website with corresponding mobile app and browser extensions that allows users to manage multiple social networks from one location, track link click-throughs and schedule future posts.

Like   The action of clicking a button on a social network, indicating that you agree, enjoy, or have seen a post or comment.

LinkedIn   A social network dedicated to professional interactions with more than 200 million users.

Mobile App   Software designed to run on smartphones, tablets, and other mobile devices that are generally created to allow users similar experiences to accessing a PC, but often with more limited functions.

Page A profile specifically for a businesses, organizations, and brands on social networks.

Pin A post on Pinterest.

Pinterest An image-based social network that allows users to "pin" pictures and videos to boards based on themes.

Post A social media update; can contain text, images, photos, and/or video.

Profile The place where a single social media user's information, photos, posts, and more appear on a social network; has its own unique URL.

Repin The action of one Pinterest user reposting another user's pin.

RSS Short for Rich Site Summary or Really Simple Syndication; a content delivery system used to publish frequently updated websites that allows readers to receive updates of new posts.

Share The act of reposting another user's post; can be text, photo, or video.

Social Media Websites that allow users to connect with each other based on shared interests and mutual connections.

Social Networks Social media that allows users to create profiles and build relationships.

Social Oomph A service that allows users to schedule posts on multiple social networks and provides additional features for measuring, analyzing, and managing posts.

Subscribe Similar to follow; the ability for a user to receive updates on other user's activity and posts without becoming "friends" or having a mutual connection on the network.

Tag   The ability to mention another social media user, making their name a link to their own profile, using the "@" sign.

Timeline   A user's profile on Facebook.

Tweet   A post on Twitter.

Twitter   A social network that allows users to quickly and concisely (140 characters or less) express things important to them and connect with other people who value the same things.

YouTube   A social network that allows users to share, comment on, and perform minor editing of videos.

Acknowledgements

The making of this book was truly a community effort. I am forever grateful to the team of people who contributed their talents in the form of ideas, time, suggestions, corrections, and encouragement.

Thank you to my mother, Katharine Washington, for always encouraging me to research and learn. Thank you to my amazing husband, CJ Martin, for his constant encouragement in this process and for the great author photo! Thank you to Karen McCullough for encouraging me to write this book and Hitaji Aziz for providing support.

I am eternally grateful to my wonderful volunteer book assassins, recruited from Facebook, whose contributions and hard work surpassed anything I expected and whose wonderful suggestions reshaped many parts of this book. Thank you: Regina Baker, Denise Bates, Alan Baumbach, Sandi Gardner, Dorita Hatchett, Monie Henderson, Kristi Jackson, Gloria Kermeen, Gary Louie, Siam Maxie, Dana Read, Misty Starks, Jody Turner, Dr. Taffy Wagner, and Connease Warren.

Thank you to my editor, Joyous Seeman, for catching my funny and not-so-funny errors.

Thank you to the hundreds of social media friends who selected the cover of this book and supported me though this entire process.

It is truly impossible to thank every single friend, family member, peer, and social media friend who contributed to this book by name, but I truly hope every single person who has contributed so much as a kind word knows how much they are appreciated.

About the Author

Major companies around the globe, including Google, Microsoft, and GE, hire Crystal Washington when they want their teams to take action online.

Crystal is known for her ability to make complex Web and social media topics easy to understand and accessible for everyday people and small business owners. As the owner of CWM Enterprises and the co-founder of Socialtunities, a social media instructional brand aimed at training everyone from Gen Y's to Baby Boomers in strategically using social media, Crystal educates consumers on the practical applications of social media networks like Facebook, Twitter, LinkedIn, and YouTube.

Crystal has been interviewed by ABC, NBC, FOX, CBS, and numerous radio stations and magazines around the globe as a social media expert. She has appeared in Black Enterprise Magazine, Black MBA Magazine, and CareerBuilder.com, and she was named one of the "Top 25 Women in Houston" in 2011.